# WIGAN
## Through Wickham's Window

Wigan parish church.

# WIGAN
## Through Wickham's Window

## A.D.Gillies
Archivist, Wigan Borough Council

## Phillimore

1988

Published by
PHILLIMORE & CO. LTD.
Shopwyke Hall, Chichester, Sussex, England

ISBN 0 85033 653 8

Printed and bound in Great Britain by
BIDDLES LTD.
Guildford, Surrey

*To the Misses Wickham*
*Cicely, Monica and Caroline*

# List of Illustrations

*Frontispiece*: Wigan parish church

## *Acknowledgements*

Appreciation is due to Metropolitan Wigan's Director of Leisure and Recreation and Amenities committee for making possible the acquisition of the Wickham photographic collection, and for granting Leonard Hudson and myself the necessary time and facilities for the preparation of this book; also to the Deputy Director of Leisure for his valued support and encouragement. I am particularly grateful to Mr. Wickham's daughters, Dr. Monica and the Misses Cicely and Caroline Wickham, for all their help and kindness, and to Mr. Kenneth Ward for his friendship and co-operation over many years; it was he who was first responsible for preserving and reproducing the Wickham photographs and, without him, the Wickham collection might well not have survived. Among many others, I wish to thank Mr. Donald Anderson of the Quaker House Colliery Co. Ltd., Mr. William Millard, grandson of James Millard, and the Rev. Richard Norburn, rector of Ampton, for all the help and advice they have so willingly given. My thanks also to my many colleagues who have given assistance, and in particular to Ann Baxter and Kerry Gee for research and typing services rendered.

This book would not have been possible without the photographic skills of Leonard Hudson, A.R.P.S., who has worked wonders in interpreting and reproducing the splendid photographs which follow. Leonard and I have worked closely together throughout the preparation of this book, and I greatly appreciate his help and advice.

Finally, I am grateful to those people who have kindly given permission for their photographs to be reproduced here: Lord Crawford, no. 129; Mr. John Hannavy, nos. 9, 67, 107, 130, 157; Mr. Jack Latham, no. 89; Mr. Len Marsden, nos. 94, 138; Mrs. Kathleen Sherrington, no. 75.

Wigan Archives Service                                                          A. D. Gillies
January 1988

## *Photographers*

**Wickham:** 2, 3, 21-48, 51, 58-62, 73, 74, 76-78, 80, 101, 103, 104, 110, 113, 115, 116, 119-26, 144, 162.

**Millard:** 4, 85, 97, 98, 131, 135, 137, 142.

**Douglas:** 19, 95, 114, 117, 118, 127, 128, 140, 141.

**Cooper:** 49, 50, 68, 70, 79, 150.

**Wragg:** 93, 105.

**Skewes:** 109, 156.

**Foley:** 16, 17.

**Crippin:** 14, 94.

**O'Reilly:** 64.

**Latham:** 136.

**Holliday:** 151.

# Introduction

Wigan – the name is bound to produce a reaction, even if many people outside the North-West have never visited the town and would be unable to pin-point it on a map. All too often the reaction is unfavourable – to some, Wigan is little more than a joke; to others, it is the archetype of the industrial northern town, symbolising the hardship, misery and degradation that affected so many of the population in the 19th and into the 20th century.

Wigan, in fact, is well-used to having a bad press. John Wesley, for example, frequently referred to wicked Wigan, a town 'proverbially famous for all manner of wickedness'. Ellen Weeton, a local governess, writing in the early 19th century, described Wigan as 'a place of mental barrenness, where ignorance and vulgarity are their boast, and literature has scarcely dawned'. In common with many, she reckoned that Wiganers had hard heads – when a coach overturned in the town, she recorded in her diary that 'many were scarcely hurt, but their heads were proof, being Wiganers. One man's head was fractured, but he came from Bolton'. More recently, George Orwell could scarcely be said to have given the town a favourable review.

But Wigan is also adept at making people change their minds. Wesley recorded that he had 'expected some disturbance. But there was none at all. A few were wild at first, but in a little while grew quiet and attentive. I did not find such a civil congregation the first time I visited Bolton.' A century later, another Methodist minister reflected that Wigan had not proved to be as bad as he expected. At first he had thought the town rather desolate-looking, 'nearly as bad as Sheffield', but he had soon found it to be 'like a beautiful garden in a thickset hedge, terrible to get through, but delightful when you get into it'.

The hitherto dubious fame given to the town by Orwell has recently been capitalised upon to great advantage at Wigan Pier; in the 1980s, more and more people are realising that Wigan is representative of all the good, as well as the bad, aspects of the northern industrial town.

There are, and always have been, two very distinct sides of the coin. Some of the photographs which follow do show squalor and hardship, and you may detect despair and suffering in some of the eyes; but far more discernible is a fierce self-respect and determination, born of a time when values and priorities were very different from those of today. These people were proud to be from Wigan.

Wigan is one of the four ancient boroughs of Lancashire, and has been a town of note for the best part of 2,000 years. The Romans made Wigan, or *Coccium* as it was then called, an important military station, on the site of the centre of the town as we know it today. The hummock at the top of Standishgate had obvious strategic advantages, and it was on the important Roman road from Warrington and Chester to the north, and close to the road from Manchester. Some years after the departure of the Romans, a group of Anglo-Saxon settlers was also attracted by the site of *Coccium* and made it into the fortified town of Wigan.

By the 13th century, Wigan was a highly prosperous town – so much so that, in 1246, Henry III saw fit to grant its first charter. The medieval borough was a walled town.

Within the walls were four principal streets – Wallgate, Standishgate, Millgate and Hallgate (the frequent use of 'gate' is a legacy of Scandinavian settlement in the tenth century), all converging on Market Place. Residence was largely restricted to freemen (members of the merchant guild) and burgesses. Strangers could enter the town, but could not stay there without the permission of the burgesses.

As a result, many immigrants and unskilled labourers, denied residence within the walls, tended to congregate in Scholes. As the walls disappeared and Wigan emerged from the Middle Ages into a more modern urban sprawl, Scholes assumed the role of the poor quarter of the town, with Woodhouses, also outside the walls, not far behind. This situation was greatly aggravated by the Industrial Revolution of the 19th century.

This, of course, was no ordinary revolution. It was, rather, the culmination of an evolution which, in the case of Wigan, can be followed over some six centuries. Coal mining, for example, certainly existed in the 14th century. By 1650, there were at least 12 commercial collieries within five miles of Wigan. The first known coalpit in the town centre was dug in Millgate in 1619. 'Back garden mining' soon became common in the town, leading to many disputes in the courts. In 1700, for example, 'Christopher Baldwin, pewterer, complained that Richard Naylor, maltster, had such a coalpit within five yards of his back door in Standishgate.' By 1771 it was claimed that, in Wigan, 'coals are in great plenty ... the coal dug up in the centre of the town is perhaps the best in the universe.' Textile manufacture records also date back to the 14th century, when three fulling mills were in operation. In time, cloth production began to emerge as a craft in its own right, carried on in the weavers' cottages. In 1784 a Cloth Hall was opened in the town, to cater for the large quantities of linens, calicoes, fustians and checks which were being produced; Wigan checks in particular were 'in much estimation'. By 1819, eight cotton mills were employing 616 people; 16 years later, there were as many as 21, as well as several corn mills. Metalworking also goes back many centuries – a pewterer, for example, is recorded in Wigan in 1470; by the 17th century, there were 250 and, after London, Wigan was probably the most important centre for pewter products in the country. Foundries produced brass, which was used in local clock and watch manufacture, bell-founding and cross-bow making. By 1788, it was claimed that 'the braziery, pewtery, brass foundry and iron forgery businesses find employment for a great number of hands'.

Then came the Industrial Revolution. For a time, the Wigan coalfield was one of the richest in the country. Coal was mined at increasingly greater depths – in the 1870s, Rose Bridge Colliery, Ince, had the deepest shafts in the country – and greater quantities. By the 1880s, some 48 colliery companies were at work in and around Wigan, producing from 5,000 up to a half a million tons per year. This was, however, at the price of female and child employment underground, until the Coalmines Regulation Act of 1842. From then on, the pit girls (the well-known pit-brow lasses) remained above ground, mainly riddling coal and shovelling it into wagons or barges.

In the mills, the power looms gradually rendered the skills of the handloom weavers obsolete and plunged many families into the depths of despair and poverty. Often a 14-hour day was worked, even by children of eight years of age, in the unhealthiest of conditions. The 1870s was a boom period for the mills, which began to dominate the skyline of the town; at times 26 spinning and weaving mills were employing up to 11,000 people.

The emphasis on engineering changed from the 1830s when developments in mining and the growth of the railways created a pressing demand for mining machinery and railway rolling stock. The Wigan Coal and Iron Company, an amalgamation of several

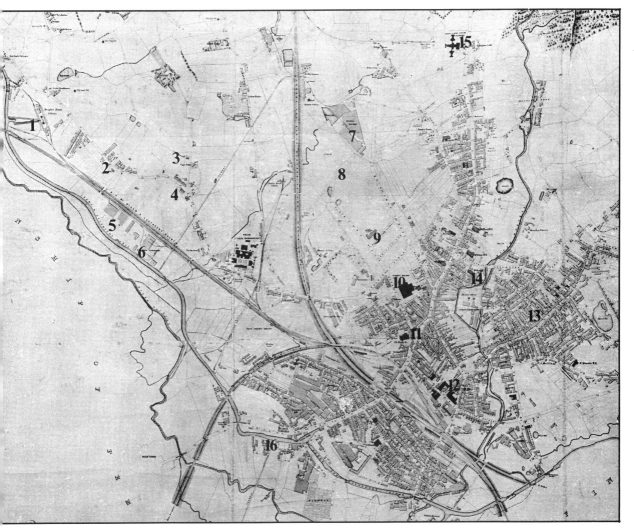

1. Wigan, in 1876, as it was when Mr. Wickham arrived. Notice the density of population in Scholes and either side of Wallgate, and the relative lack of development around St Andrew's. Douglas Bank Colliery and Pagefield Ironworks, however, were already flourishing, and when Mr. Wickham left Wigan the rapid spread of urbanisation had made St Andrew's an integral part of the town.

## KEY

| | | | |
|---|---|---|---|
| 1. | Douglas Bank Colliery | 9. | Wigan Grammar School |
| 2. | Woodhouse Lane, where Mr. Wickham took most of his photographs | 10. | Market Hall and Square |
| 3. | St Andrew's church and vicarage | 11. | Wigan parish church |
| 4. | Pagefield Loco Brickworks | 12. | Wigan Public Library |
| 5. | Wigan Rolling Mills | 13. | Scholes |
| 6. | Pagefield Ironworks | 14. | St George's church |
| 7. | Rylands Mill | 15. | Royal Albert Edward Infirmary |
| 8. | Mesnes Park | 16. | Wigan Pier |

existing collieries and ironworks, was one of the country's largest firms by the 1880s, while Walker Brothers' Pagefield Ironworks would become world-famous for its mining machinery.

These vast changes, however, brought with them unprecedented social disruption and hardship. Between 1801 and 1851 Wigan's population increased ten-fold to 40,000, somehow accommodated in hundreds of houses crammed into any yard or open ground available, resulting in a multitude of courts, terraces and back-to-backs. William Dodd, who visited Wigan in 1841, wrote of 'heaps of accumulated filth' and could not recall 'ever to have seen so much misery and wretchedness in such a small compass before'. A report of 1845 referred to 5,366 houses in the town, of which 4,264 were of 'working class type'; 1,649 were back-to-back, 647 others were without windows at the back, while 60 were cellar dwellings. It was reported that there were 27 slaughter houses in residential areas, as well as 38 lodging houses, half of which were in areas described as seats of fever.

Particularly unpleasant seems to have been Barrack Square (off what is now Library Street) – it was described as 'ill-drained, ill-paved and a seat of fever ... 45 cottages in a very confined situation, no thoroughfare and closed up at the bottom. They are very small with the ground floors below ground level with four privies – all in the dirtiest and filthiest state – serving 45 cottages with 257 inhabitants. It is neither lit nor supplied with water. The yard is always poorly drained, dirty and smells.' A contemporary observer described the Scholes Little Ireland area as 'the ash pit of human life' with 'bye streets of mean brick cottages, with unwholesome downcast look – sallow tattered women, lounging in the doorways, listlessly watching their sickly children in the street. The very children seemed joyless in their play.'

The lack of an adequate supply of water was a particular problem. Most Wiganers were dependent on streams, springs and wells – up to 10,000 on the Boy's Well alone – which had become heavily polluted, and real progress in providing a proper piped water supply was not made until the 1860s. The house drainage and sewerage systems of the mid-19th century were unbelievably primitive. Sewage was often left to accumulate in open cesspools or ditches, as less than 20% of the total length of the town's streets were sewered, and even these sewers either discharged into the Douglas or into open ditches around the town. Not until 1874 was a proper sewerage system adopted.

As the population increased, so did the number of public houses. Even as early as 1634, Wigan had 51 inns, situated as it was on the great north road. But by the 1860s, there were 110 public houses and 80 beer-sellers. By 1878, there were over 300 ale-houses, 70 of which were in Scholes alone – virtually one at every street corner. With houses open from early morning until late at night, and porter costing only 3d. a quart, drunkenness was rife.

In contrast, the Primitive Methodists in particular led the fight against the evils of strong drink, through the formation of temperance societies such as the Band of Hope, and sought to popularise tea, 'the cup that cheers but not inebriates'. The churches also, of course, had another daunting task, to meet the spiritual needs of the masses. One Church of England vicar who strove valiantly to fulfil these tasks was William Wickham.

The Wigan of 1878 must have been something of a culture shock to Mr. Wickham. He had been born in 1849 in Trowbridge, Wiltshire, where he received his schooling. After a number of years of teaching he entered Lichfield Theological College in 1873. The following year, he continued his northern progression by taking up his first clerical appointment as curate in the Staffordshire village of Talke-o'-th'-Hill. In a sense, then, the move further north to Lancashire was a natural step but, when Canon Bridgeman, rector of Wigan, offered him Wigan St Andrew's, he had reservations, as he had another

2.   Mr. Wickham, the family man, 1900. He married Clara Peck, L.R.A.M., in 1892. The children are, from left to right, Bernard (b. 1894), Cicely (b. 1896), Caroline (b. 1899), Myrtle (b. 1893), and Monica (b. 1898). Lieutenant Bernard Wickham was killed on active service near Ypres in 1917. Cicely, Monica and Caroline still live in Hampshire. Mr. Wickham may well have taken this photograph himself, by delayed action.

offer to consider as well. As he was to tell his congregation, this other living was 'much richer and far more comely than you are. Taking into consideration the perpetual fogs and smoke, the constant floods, the long rows of cottages, the roads which remind one more of swamp tracks rather than of streets of an ancient borough, the gas which has such a power of making darkness visible that it would almost turn day into night if it were allowed to burn – no-one will accuse you of being too handsome. Well, I will tell you that it was your very poverty and lack of beauty which drew my heartstrings towards you.'

3. Mr. Wickham surveys his parish through the vicarage window. Photograph 29 shows the view he would have seen.

Mr. Wickham's choice had not been an easy one. As with so many before him, and after, he came with certain preconceived ideas – Wigan was associated with 'bad railway accidents, colliery explosions and monster strikes'. Nor were his first impressions anyway favourable. He was later to recall how, as he arrived in Wigan for the first time, a fellow train-passenger exclaimed, 'O, what place is this? What an 'orrible place'. And, he confessed, 'that is about what I thought myself. I used to get letters of condolence from my friends. The first few months of my life here were certainly very trying, but when the summer weather came and I found out the Standish woods, I began to change my mind.' And so began a love-affair which was to last for 38 years. Even today, Mr. Wickham's three surviving daughters remember happy days in the Standish woods, where their father walked and played with them, and wrote his sermons; and although they left Wigan in 1916, they still proudly call themselves Wiganers.

Mr. Wickham soon settled into his new environment and, before long, was extolling the virtues of that well-known Lancashire institution, the clog. 'In a pair of clogs a man, or woman either, may feel superior to all mud, cold or snow. The clogged foot is certain to be dry and warm. With no other foot covering can you make as much noise on a stone pavement. A dozen clogged feet on the street of a southern town would almost persuade the shivering inhabitants that the horrors of war were at their front doors.' Although able to manage clogs, Mr. Wickham told his parishioners, 'when it comes to the dialect I have to confess myself beaten. It is altogether beyond me. I look with reverence upon a man who can converse freely and easily in broad Lancashire. I regard him also with a hopeless envy.'

Mr. Wickham has, in fact, left us a marvellous record, written as well as pictorial, of life in Wigan at a time when it was coming to terms with the effects of the Industrial Revolution and moving into the 20th century. He arrived at a momentous time – Mesnes Park and the Public Library were opened in the same year; the Market Hall and Market Square had been opened only the year before, and the Royal Albert Edward Infirmary in 1873. Much of the old Wigan, however, remained until well into the present century, and there can be no better description than Mr. Wickham's evocative lament over the plight of St George's church in the early 1900s.

> The west door freely admits the many noises of the cobble-paved and clog-trodden streets. On the north side is a private road leading to an old cotton factory which has stood idle for 30 years, and is in ruins. Not far away is a good-sized manure heap, and a couple of years ago, there was a van-dweller, a travelling hawker and horse-dealer, who made the yard his headquarters, and used to exercise his horses on a Sunday morning on the road along the north side of the church. On the other side of this road is a wheelwright's shop, with its cheerful sounds, and sometimes its concentrated black smoke especially troublesome when a wheel is being 'hooped', and a north wind is blowing. A small passage runs round the church on the north and east sides. Dark tales are told of evil uses to which this neighbourhood of the church is sometimes put. There is a slaughter-house about 20 yards to the south. The cries of the animals sometimes became urgent. The scents from the south are what might be expected from such a south. The yard on the south side is used by children of the neighbourhood as a very convenient playground.

Such a marvellously evocative description is bettered only by some 200 splendid photographs of Wigan which Mr. Wickham took in the early 1890s. In all, he took over 1,000 images – some during his student days, of Hampshire, Devon, Yorkshire and Scotland, some in Switzerland, which he visited on several occasions and where he spent his honeymoon – but these are all the subject of another book. Here, we are concerned with those he took of Wigan, and in particular of the people in his own parish, often within a stone's throw of the church and vicarage, a veritable microcosm, in fact, of Wigan at the end of the 19th century.

We see the streets of terraced houses, the back-to-backs, the yards, the men at work and in their homes, the women engaged in their domestic duties, the street-traders and, best of all, life at the colliery. Mr. Wickham was one of the first in the country to take flash photographs underground, a feat which can hardly have been achieved without a certain element of danger. Moreover, many of his Douglas Bank Colliery views were taken as a series, probably on the same day, to illustrate the daily life of the collier.

Using his bellows-type camera and dry plates, Mr. Wickham would take a glass plate negative, from which he then made a contact print, approximately 4in. x 3in. But he also made lantern slides of most, if not all, of his Wigan photographs. These were taken for use in lantern slide shows, to raise money to pay off the building costs of his church school. He had already made considerable use of commercial slides for devotional purposes, and also for educational and recreational use. After giving a well-received show at the Infirmary, he reflected, 'more might be done than is done to amuse the patients. A little interest excited or a good laugh is often as good as a dose of physic to a recovering invalid. The nurses too have a somewhat monotonous life, and an occasional entertainment would brighten it up a little.' In October 1891, he projected his own slides for the first time.

The Public Hall, King Street, was packed with an audience which included 'most of the gentry of the town, and the miners were very much in evidence', although Mr. Wickham had warned that 'the thing we want to avoid is cramming the room so full that no one will be able to laugh'. By all accounts, when they saw themselves on the big screen, Wiganers did have a good laugh. *The Wigan Examiner* reported that 'much amusement was caused by the representation of a collier's daily life' and that the photographs taken in the pit were 'certainly the tit-bit of the exhibition, and many wondered how the photographs could have been obtained 'deawn th' pit'.'

Mr. Wickham repeated the show twice the following month, by popular demand and, during the colliers' strike of 1893, he took a few more photographs. These, however, were effectively the last of any historical interest for Wigan. Increasing family and parish responsibilities meant that, unfortunately for us, he could no longer afford the time for anything other than family snapshots. By 1916, he was 67 years of age, tired, and in declining health. He even allowed himself a rare quibble with the Almighty, 'I have often reverently wondered why God, who helped me so wonderfully in other directions, willed that I should be single-handed when there was ample work for two priests'. The time had come to take things easier, and he and his family moved to the sleepy little Suffolk village of Ampton, where he remained rector until his death in 1929.

The non-Wickham photographs reproduced here were mainly taken by 'professionals'. In many cases we know the photographer, but in others we do not, and probably never will. Of those that can be identified, four are of particular note. John Cooper, for example, combined his photographic work with that of landlord for over 30 years, only working exclusively on his photographic business from the mid-1890s. Before then, he had studios in the *Royal Oak* and *Green Man*, both in Standishgate, and in the *Harrogate Inn*, Harrogate Street. Cooper tended to concentrate less and less on portrait photography (which he left to his wife) and more on architectural photography, and was regularly commissioned by the Corporation to record the changing face of Wigan. So, too, was Rudolph Douglas, who operated from 23 Upper Dicconson Street. Herbert Wragg had his studio at 45 Mesnes Street (now a part of Smith's Bookshop) for much of our period; he was essentially a portrait photographer.

Finally, perhaps the most interesting of all the professional photographers of the period was James Millard. Like Cooper, he had various interests apart from photography – he was also an optician, picture framer and hardware dealer, among other things. Also like Cooper, he had various studios during a long career (*c*.1870 to *c*.1920), including several in Market Street. One of these, on the site now occupied by the Queen's Hall, is of particular interest, as two photographs of it survive, one of which is reproduced here. Moreover, this and another two photographs also included in this book portray James Millard himself – virtually the only known views of a Victorian Wigan photographer and studio.

Taken together, the photographs which follow show Wigan through Wickham's window, be it through the lens of his or of another camera, but as he would have seen it with his own eyes. We have a mixture of amateur and professional photographs, of views of the parish church of St Andrew's and of the centre of the town, and of faces and street scenes – the whole showing Wigan as it emerged from the upheaval of the Industrial Revolution and entered the 20th century.

4.  Wigan photographer James Millard, *c.*1915, with the sculpture of a mill-girl, with shuttle, which he had made himself. This sculpture was one of two which had flanked his studio in Market Street (*see* photograph 98). This photograph was probably taken by his son William, who followed in his father's footsteps.

The photographs, although not divided into sections, nevertheless follow a certain pattern. Where better to begin than with churches and church life? All the major denominations are represented. After all, Wigan has long enjoyed a tradition of high church attendance, whatever the denomination. But even with a virtually full church, Mr. Wickham could still bemoan the fact that the allotment gardens close to the church, 'though they may to some extent keep the men out of the public house, do not aid in bringing them to church'. What would he say if he were alive today?

The numbers attending Sunday School were phenomenal by today's standards, yet there was widespread absenteeism from day-school. Mr. Wickham summed up the dangers: 'a child who is allowed to be irregular at school will spend a good deal of time in the streets, and when there, he will acquire irregular habits, which in many cases will stick to him through life, to his great disadvantage.' Many of those children who did attend school were part-timers. As James Millard's son, George, a Pemberton teacher, recalled, 'some of the children worked at May Mill; they started at 5.30 a.m. and worked until dinner time. They came to school in the afternoon, and the poor things would fall asleep on their desks; the teachers used to waken them up with the cane.'

Looking out through his vicarage window, we can see the industrialized landscape with which Mr. Wickham would have been familiar. In the distance, he could see the Douglas Bank Colliery. He has left us with a marvellous insight into Victorian Wigan colliery working life – and non-working life, too. In 1893, the Miners' Federation of Great Britain called a strike against a proposed reduction of 25% in wages; the men were out for 16 weeks, from 28 July to 7 November.

These were days of great privation amongst the working population. One local church worker recalled how, during a visit to a collier's house, 'what I saw then cut me to the heart. The family numbered eight; they were having dinner when I called, and the meal consisted of seven potatoes – seven potatoes for eight persons!' A soup kitchen, one of many in the town, was manned by St Andrew's church members for as long as possible, and Mr. Wickham took his turn at serving. He also gave lantern shows for the miners and, on a separate evening, their wives and daughters – 'the women seemed greatly to enjoy the show, and made twice as much noise as the men. This may perhaps be partly accounted for by the fact that their mouths had no pipes in them'. But as funds became exhausted and winter approached, he wrote, 'whoever is responsible for the continuance of the strike will have something to answer for. The prospect is indeed gloomy, and the strain on people is greater. We can only say, "God help us".' When the dreadful strike was finally over, 'our first feeling was one of deep thankfulness. But who has won? Both sides have lost. The masters have lost. They demanded a reduction, but the men have gone back to work on the old terms. But have the men won? 16 weeks' wages have been lost. Is this much of a victory? It will take many a long month to get over even some of those losses; some never can be got over.'

The housing and hygiene conditions depicted in this book show some improvement from the earlier part of the century, as the problems of water supply, drainage, sewage disposal and sanitation began to be overcome. The arrival of the tram in particular facilitated further ribbon development of property along or near the main roads. Nevertheless, the report of the Medical Officer of Health for 1899 listed just 1,685 water closets, and 8,630 pail-closets. He recommended that 'water-closets be substituted for the present privy accommodation in all those houses from which at the present time the contents have to be wheeled out along passages, and deposited in front streets before removal.' In December 1901, Mr. Wickham reported that his parish had of late been suffering from typhoid fever – 16 cases during a few months. 'The wonder is that we have not had more of it, for beyond the Douglas Bank Colliery Offices there is no main sewer. Moreover, the sanitary arrangements of many of the older homes are almost as bad as they can be.'

The situation was further aggravated by a continued rise in population – that of St Andrew's, for example, doubled, to 2,000, in the last quarter of the 19th century. Mr. Wickham warned his congregation of the dangers of overcrowding, especially in bedrooms. 'It is morally very injurious and also injurious to health. We each of us need a certain space of air in which to breathe. If we have less than this we breathe in again the carbonic acid gas we have previously breathed out. The result is perhaps only a headache, or it may be, as in Michael Carney's case, death by asphyxia.' Carney, an ironworker's labourer, lived in a two-bedroomed house in Scholes, one of four lodgers, along with the owner's family of seven. The coroner reported that 'there were four persons in the back room where the deceased was, and it had only accommodation for two, with regard to the allowance of air.' Mr. Wickham concluded, 'we cannot neglect the laws of health and get off scot-free.'

As the population increased, so did the number of public houses. Mr. Wickham bemoaned the fact that 'there are nine drinkshops of various sorts in the parish, and these are a great hindrance'. One Sunday morning after church, he saw 'a knot of over 50 men standing outside one of those miserable drinkshops which here as elsewhere are the curse of the place. There they stood dirty and disreputable-looking.' On returning from convalescence on the continent, Mr. Wickham reflected 'we never saw a man or woman drunk. How different from Wigan!'

Not that those in employment had an abundance of leisure time – what they had they earned, and they generally used it to the full. Circuses were a highlight. Particularly popular were Wombwell's circus, which had many wild animals, and Mander's Wild Beast Menagerie. A visit to the fair meant peep shows, magic lantern shows, sideshows, and exhibitions of freaks. Theatres and music halls were usually packed. Wigan, of course, has a strong sporting tradition, including clog-fighting, which remained popular well into this century. Combatants, often naked apart from their clogs, would kick their opponent, be he standing or fallen; women were said to form the majority in the audiences! It is unlikely that Mr. Wickham would have approved of clogs being used in this way.

The final photograph in this book is, appropriately, of Mr. Wickham himself, the one with which he finished his lantern shows. He bade farewell to Wigan in 1916 – the end of an era in many ways. He left in the midst of the Great War, after which things could never be the same again. The depression of the 1920s was just around the corner and the heyday of many Wigan industries was over. A new Wigan would soon emerge, one which would be very different from that which Mr. Wickham knew. His parting words to his congregation were, 'remember that when I depart you will have done with the old vicar; in all probability you will never see him again, though I do not think you will at once forget him.' I hope that this book will ensure that, over 70 years later, both he and the Wigan he knew and loved are still not forgotten.

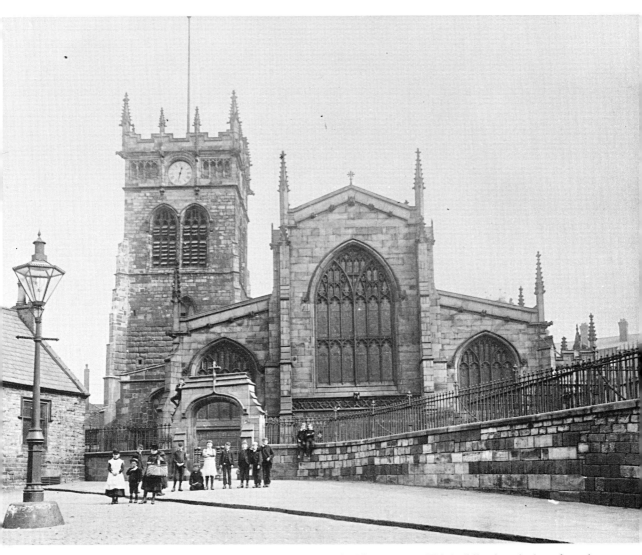

5.   Wigan parish church, from the corner of Bishopgate and Crawford Street, 1892. This building largely dates from the period 1845-50, when the church was almost entirely rebuilt on the style of its predecessor; the 13th-century lower parts of the tower, however, remain. Between 1898 and 1902 the whole of the exterior stonework was restored.

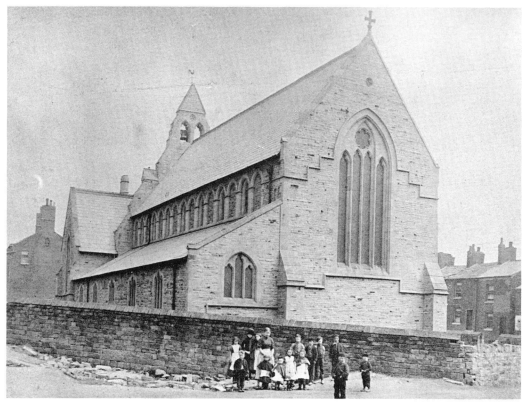

6.   St Michael and All Angels' church, 1882. Designed by the eminent Victorian architect, George Street, this church had been built four years earlier, as a chapel-of-ease for the Swinley area. It became a parish church in 1881.

7.   Wigan's first Presbyterian church, Chapel Lane. Built in 1769, it was popularly known as the Scotch Chapel. It was for a time the only orthodox Presbyterian place of worship in Lancashire. This photograph was taken shortly before its demolition in 1876, when it was replaced by a much more impressive building, with Gothic façade and spire.

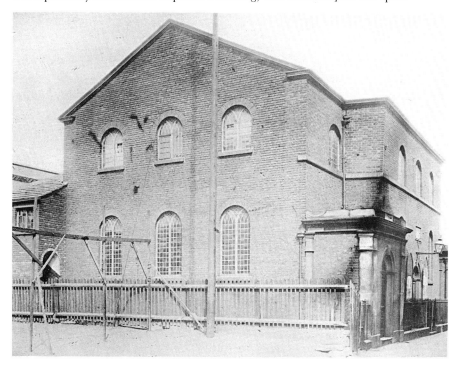

8. (*right*) Central Hall, Station Road. Primitive Methodism in Wigan dates back to 1822, but this superb building, erected in 1898, was its first permanent home. The cost was high – £3,320 – and it took many years to pay off the debt. Frequent bazaars were held to help raise money and competitions were run, including 'Men's Face Washing' and 'Straight Face for Young Ladies'.

9. (*below*) St John's Roman Catholic church Walking Day, 1912, Standishgate. This was always a highlight in the church calendar. On this particular occasion, due to a shortage of Morris dancers, the local lads apparently had to dress, if not actually play, the part.

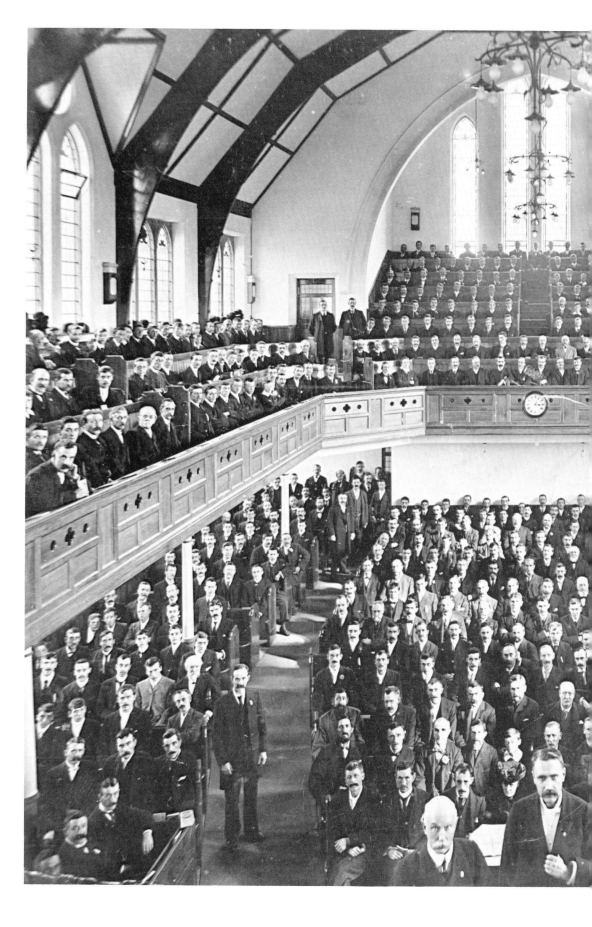

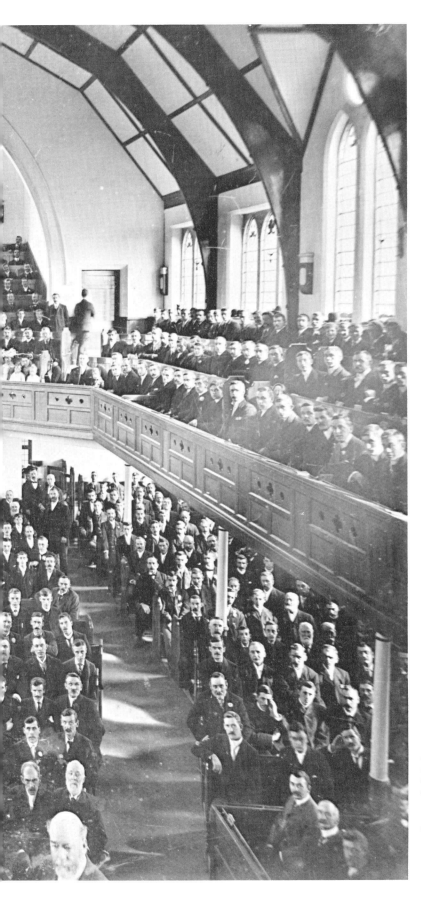

10.  St Paul's Congregational church, Standishgate, P.S.A. (Pleasant Sunday Afternoon), 1903. The original church, built in 1785, was demolished in 1902 and the new church, on the same site,was opened the following year. The P.S.A. donated a new organ, and this photograph was presumably taken at its inauguration. The P.S.A. was for men only – but a few women still managed to be present!

1867

| Nov. 12th | Exchanged the Table for a proper Teachers' Desk. |
| " 13th | Rev. F. Crozier, the Secretary of Committee called. |
| " 14th | Very wet could not go out to play. |
| " 15th | Av. Att! for Week = 120 |
| " x | No. pres. at all = 130 |
| " 18th | A scholar who was present last week died on Sat.y night of Scarlet Fever. |
| " 19th | Bible Lesson - "Parable of Sower" |
| " 20th | Exc.d II St. in Arith. - find they must revise Notation and the Tables. |
| " 21st | Another Scholar died to-day - which |
| " | makes 6 altogether |
| " 22nd | Av. att. for Week - 123 |
| | No. pres. at All = 135 |
| " 25th | Bible Lesson - John the Baptist |
| " | beheaded. |
| " 26th | Exc.d Arithmetic of II St. |

11.   Extract from Ince Wesleyan School log book, November 1867. Two entries refer to the deaths of scholars. Other problems included the weather and the parents; often it was 'too cold to write in copy books', while parents were 'of the low collier class, proverbial for their improvident habits. The greatest enemies many of these children have are their parents.'

12. Infant class, Dicconson Street Wesleyan Day School, 1913. Despite the inadequacy of the premises to cope with the demands of the 20th century, remarkable successes were achieved, and such was the reputation of the school that it survived until 1967. One well-known Wigan personality, Miss Joan Bamford, M.B.E., L.R.A.M., L.T.C.L., is seated underneath the Maypole.

13. Infant class, National and Bluecoat School, Hallgate, *c.*1914. The Infants' School was opened in 1867, next door to the Bluecoat School which had moved there in 1825.

14. 'Never Absent', 1898 – Class I, National and Bluecoat Infants' School, Hallgate.

15.  The Manor House Boarding School, Bishopgate, 1861. Originally, this had been a house built by John Walmesley in the second half of the 17th century. Bonnie Prince Charlie reputedly spent the night of 10 December 1745 there, during his retreat north, and his pursuer, the Duke of Cumberland, the following night. The building was demolished *c*.1930.

16.  The Girls' High School, Standishgate, *c*.1907. Following the condemnation of the first High School, opened in 1887 opposite the rectory, the school moved here in 1906 for about a year, before it moved again, to the 'Tin Tabernacle', a temporary structure built behind the School House. This was replaced by the new High School.

17.   Laying the foundation stone for the new Girls' High School, Standishgate, 3 March 1915. At its opening, the Headmistress, Miss Banks, compared her position with that of the old woman who lived in a shoe: she had so many children she did not know what to do. She now had 250 girls, and already she could not accommodate them all. The school is now Mabs Cross Primary School.

18.   The former Wigan Grammar School. Founded in 1597, the original building was at School Common, Scholes. In 1723, a new school was built on the present site of the Central Library. The building shown here, opened in 1879, was the third, 'a model of what a school building ought to be'. The current building, on the same site, replaced it in 1936.

19. Wigan and District Mining and Technical College, Library Street, 1903. This photograph was taken soon after the opening of the building by the Countess of Crawford. In 1857, Wigan had become only the second town in the country to establish a Mining School, also in Library Street. This was incorporated in the splendid new red brick and terracotta building.

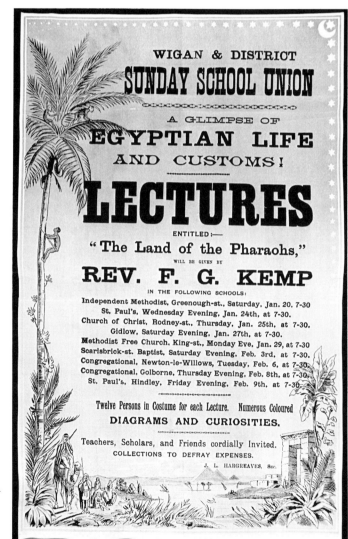

20. Wigan and District Sunday School Union lectures, 1894. The Union comprised all evangelical Sunday Schools and organised regular meetings, exhibitions and excursions (*see* photograph 134). In 1896, an Eisteddfod was introduced, with essays, recitations and music by children of all ages.

21.   The odd-jobman and cleaner, St Andrew's church, 1891. The former is holding a carpenter's adze.

22.   Members of St Andrew's Mothers' Meeting, 1891. This group met regularly on Thursday afternoons.

23. St Andrew's church and vicarage, c.1897. Mr. Wickham had to hold his services at Martland Bridge School until 1882, when the church was finally completed. He was without a vicarage, however, for nearly 20 years, until he and his family at last moved early in 1897. His verdict was, 'a substantial, convenient, windswept and sunny building'.

24. Members of St Andrew's Bible Class, 1891. This class usually met on Friday evenings, led by Mr. Wickham himself. John House, manager of Douglas Bank Colliery, relieved him for a short time but, when he had to resign, the indefatigable Mr. Wickham took over once again.

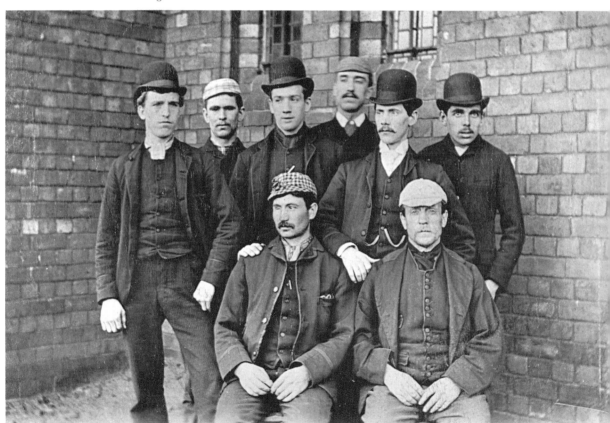

25.  Some of the parishioners who helped man the St Andrew's soup kitchen, during the miners' strike in 1893. The strike lasted from 28 July to 7 November. A central fund helped to finance various soup kitchens, including that at St Andrew's which opened on 25 August. By the time money ran out in October, some 17,000 dinners had been served.

26.  Anxious, but resolute, faces.

27.  St Andrew's soup kitchen. Each day, some 350 needy children were provided with a dinner.

28. Mr. Wickham himself was quite prepared to lend a hand serving soup.

29. (*above*) The view through Mr. Wickham's vicarage window, *c.*1898. In the distance, he could see the Douglas Bank Colliery, by far the most distinctive feature of St Andrew's parish. Just over the vicarage walls was the brickworks. In between the two ran rows of tightly-packed back-to-backs. In effect, a microcosm of Wigan.

30. (*opposite*) A closer view of the Douglas Bank Colliery, 1891. The two identical tall chimneys were a distinctive feature; in the middle was the furnace chimney. Mr. Wickham would have taken this photograph from the other side of the Leeds-Liverpool canal.

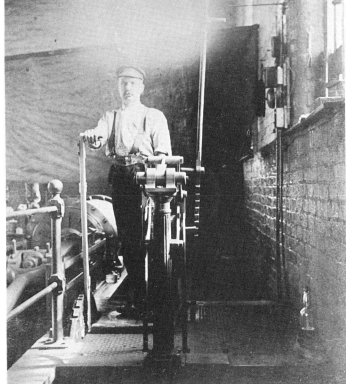

31. (*right*) The beginning of the shift at Douglas Bank Colliery, showing the winder in the winding room, operating a Daglish winding machine. The colliery had two shafts, each 1,971ft. deep. In the north pit, cages were wound from 1,971ft. and 1,797ft., and in the south pit, from 1,125ft. and 543ft.

32. & 33.  Mr. Wickham was one of the first in the country to take photographs underground, a remarkable achievement for 'a beginner', as he called himself. These photographs show a collier getting the coal and a drawer helping with the filling of the tubs (*above*), and a drawer pushing a tub to the main haulage (*below*). The lamp and tub are typical of the Wigan collieries.

34. (*right*) Colliers in the cage, returning to the surface at the end of the shift. A message for the banksman can be seen. The same cage, with minimum protection, was used for men and tubs alike; a special signal, however, was given when men were travelling, and the winder raised or lowered the cage more carefully.

35. (*left*) Back to the surface and the banksman pulls a loaded tub out of the cage. This, in fact, was somewhat unusual – normally, the loaded tubs would be pushed rather than pulled out.

36. (*above*) A tub being weighed, while another is pushed off. In the centre is the tally-boy. In the weigh-house are the weighman, appointed by the company, and the check-weighman, chosen by the men or the Union.

37. (*left*) A lampman is flanked by the blacksmith on the left and the carpenter on the right. Notice the moleskin breeches.

38. (*above*) Locomotive *Ince* outside the
Lancashire and Yorkshire Railway sheds. This
was originally an Ince Hall Coal and Cannel
Company engine, before being transferred to
Douglas Bank.

39. (*right*) Pit-brow lasses shovelling coal into
a wagon. In 1878, Arthur Munby, after a visit
to Douglas Bank Colliery, had written of 'girls
thrutching [pushing] full corves [baskets] from
the pit shaft ... girls with their spades standing
in the holds of barges, girls standing in the
railing trucks under the belts, arranging coal
with their hands as each load came thundering
down.'

40. Loading blocks of cannel. The Wigan coalfield was particularly noted for its high-quality cannel, which made good fires without ashes and with only a little smoke, produced a long-lived brilliant flame, and was highly suited to gas production. There was a 3ft. seam of cannel at Douglas Bank.

41. & 42. Pit-brow lasses tipping tubs of coal over fixed screens, which in turn fed the waiting barges in the canal basin below.

43. (*left*) Emptying 'dirt' from a dead buffer wagon. These wagons were not allowed on the main line from the late 19th century.

44. (*below*) Pit-brow lasses queueing for their pay. In the 1890s, Wigan had over 800 pit girls. Many wore trousers thus attracting particularly adverse publicity, and increasing demands for female surface labour to come to an end. By the late 1960s, there were no pit-brow lasses left in Lancashire though the last female surface worker in Britain was not made redundant until 1972.

45. Colliers' pay queue. The camera was obviously a source of considerable fascination and amusement.

46. Another view of Douglas Bank Colliery, 1891, showing how quickly the scene could change! The colliery closed down in 1921, and the Walker Fan, installed in 1903, was transferred to Alexandra Pit, Haigh.

47. (*left*) Loading hay near Douglas Bank, 1891.

48. (*below*) A splendid view of an early threshing machine at work, again near Douglas Bank in 1891.

49. An old corn mill, Coppull Lane, *c.*1900, one of several in or near the town.

50. Handloom weavers' cottages, Wigan Lane, 1904. These were typical of many which housed Wigan's weaving looms in the 18th and 19th centuries, before the power looms rendered the skills of the handloom weavers obsolete. Notice how the cellars have become small shops. The site of these houses is now occupied by Swinley Labour Club.

51.  Mill girls with snap baskets and cans, 1891. So far as is known, this splendid view is the only one of mill girls which Mr. Wickham took.

52. A group of mill girls with shuttles, *c.*1900. Many enjoyed the friendly atmosphere and camaraderie; yet when a local doctor contrasted pit-brow lasses and mill girls, he concluded that he would rather marry one of the former because, despite the harsher demands of the job, they did not have to work in the warm, damp, noisy atmosphere of the cotton mill.

53. Coop's Factory, Dorning Street. Timothy Coop, a Wallgate tailor in the 1860s, believed that the future for clothing manufacture lay in large factories. This purpose-built factory was opened in 1872; 500 people were employed, on a nine-hour work system which was highly revolutionary for the time. Coop and Co. also had a retail outlet at nos. 1 and 3 Wallgate (*see* photograph 90).

54.   The workforce at Clarington Forge, Darlington Street East, on the Wigan/Ince boundary. William Park had established a forge here as early as 1789. In 1929, a subsidiary of William Park & Co., English Tools Limited, was set up here, producing a range of industrial and agricultural hand tools, such as shovels, rakes, bill hooks, picks and hammers.

55.   William Park & Co. iron and steel warehouse, the Wiend, c.1901. This store was not transferred to Clarington Forge until 1950.

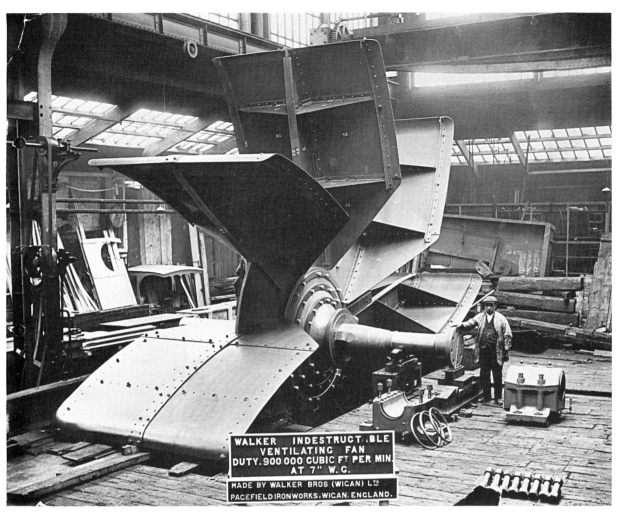

Text on image:

WALKER INDESTRUCTIBLE
VENTILATING FAN
DUTY. 900,000 CUBIC F⊥ PER MIN.
AT 7" W.G.
MADE BY WALKER BROS (WIGAN) L⊤ᴰ
PAGEFIELD IRONWORKS, WIGAN, ENGLAND.

56.  The Pagefield Ironworks was founded in 1873. From 1904, it was known as Walker Brothers (Wigan) Ltd. The company became a leading manufacturer of mining machinery and general engineering products; probably most famous was the Indestructible Fan, which was used to ventilate mines, not just throughout Britain, but in such countries as South Africa, India, Japan, Russia, Mexico, Canada and Australia.

57.  From the beginning, Walker Brothers sought to diversify and, for 50 years, the company manufactured cars and goods vehicles. Two cars were produced as early as 1904, and the first lorry in 1907, bought by the well-known firm of O. & G. Rushton. The lorry shown here, outside the former Wigan Grammar School, was produced c.1920; the agent's name will be familiar to all Wiganers.

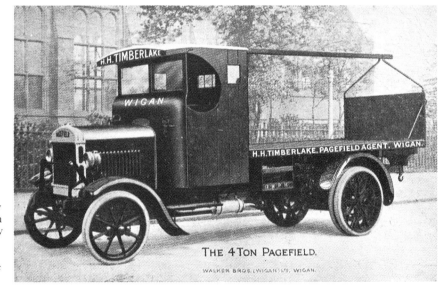

Text on image:

H.H.TIMBERLAKE
WIGAN
H.H.TIMBERLAKE, PAGEFIELD AGENT. WIGAN.
THE 4 TON PAGEFIELD.
WALKER BROS. (WIGAN) Lⁿ. WIGAN.

58. Wigan Rolling Mills, 1891 – the shingler at work. Balls of wrought iron from the puddling furnace would be taken to the steam hammer and shingled, or hammered, to consolidate and weld together the particles of iron, expel surplus cinder, and shape them into a rectangular bloom, ready to be rolled.

59. The head roller (*right*) and millmen, Wigan Rolling Mills, 1891. Once the wrought-iron balls had been shingled into blooms, they were passed, while still hot, to the rolling mill, where they would be rolled several times and made into all sorts of shapes.

60. The shingler (*right*) and his mate. As shingling expelled large quantities of molten cinder, the shingler had to wear protective clothing. This included sheet iron foot and shin guards, a heavy leather apron and, as can be seen in photograph 58, a wire gauze face mask.

61. & 62.  The Pagefield Loco
Brickworks, Woodhouse Lane, 1891. The
works was just outside St Andrew's
vicarage wall (*see* photograph 29). It was
common for a brickworks to be situated
near a colliery, as the shale and fireclay
found there were particularly suitable for
the purpose. The bricks seen here,
produced from boulder clay, were mainly
used for house-building.

63. (*above*) Henry Farr & Son, carriage builders, *c.*1900. These premises were situated at the corner of Market Street and Woodcock Street, adjoining the Commercial Hall. As can be seen from the notice, this photograph was taken shortly after the firm had moved to new premises at nos. 129 and 133 Wallgate. The poster on the left refers to the evil of bigamy!

64. (*right*) A new wagon, built by William Moss & Sons, wagon builders, wheelwrights and blacksmiths. This firm began business at no. 220 Woodhouse Lane, but around 1888 moved to Orchard Street. Henry Atherton & Sons, boiled sweet manufacturers, had premises in Mesnes Street and Market Street, as well as Scholefield Lane, Hallgate and Wigan Lane; the sons were also involved in the entertainment business (*see* photograph 159).

65.  The interior of William Kenyon
& Sons, wheelwrights and coffin
makers, no. 57 Darlington Street. The
firm was established in 1880 and
during the Great War had a
government contract to make artillery
wheels.

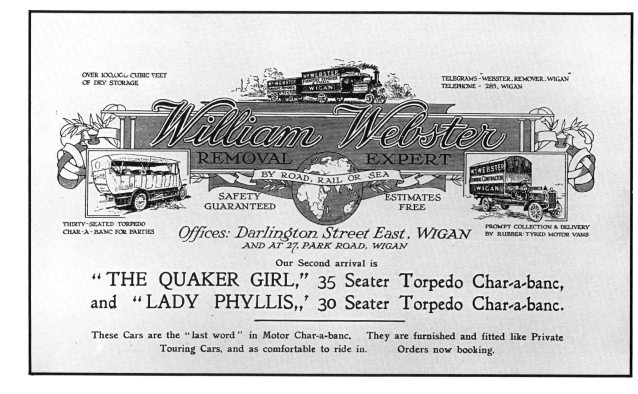

66. & 67. William Webster began work as a miner, but reverted to selling coal once he had saved enough money to buy a horse and cart. He then opened a furniture removal and coach service, with premises at no. 190 Darlington Street East. The Excelsior Steam Wagon (*below*) was built by the Foden Steam Wagon Co. and was one of the first such vehicles in Wigan. It could travel at six m.p.h. on solid metal tyres, and weighed just under five tons, empty! Each morning, it took an hour to get up steam!

58. Miles Williams & Co., paint and varnish manufacturers, Britannia Varnish Works, Scholes Bridge, *c*.1895. A retail shop was situated on the premises and the firm had another branch in Bootle.

59. Billhead, William Livesey, 23 Queen Street, 1913. This large site, near the Wallgate end of Queen Street, is now occupied by Coalite Building Supplies. The large title-board on the left of the illustration can still, however, be seen.

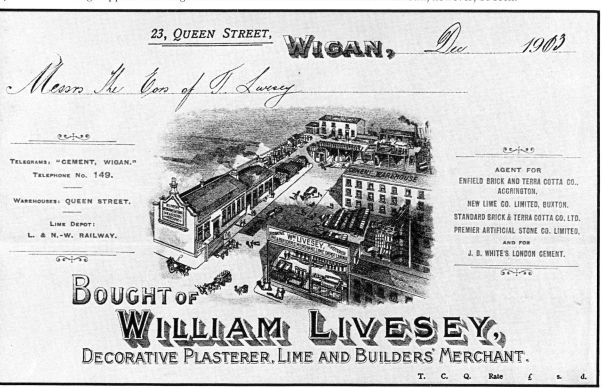

70. Farrington's clogger's shop, nos. 73 and 75 Wigan Lane, *c*.1893. James Farrington had earlier owned a small shop at the corner of Coppull Lane (no. 87). To the left is James Jackson's butcher's shop (with slaughter house behind), Ashton's clogger's shop and the *Saracen's Head*. The alleyway between Jackson's and Farrington's led to Rainford Buildings.

71. Wigan Lane shops, 1872. This view is almost a direct continuation of the photograph above. Three shops separated th *Saracen's Head* (above) from one corner of Coppull Lane. Alice Crook's grocer's and baker's shop (no. 89) was at the other corner. The sign above the left-hand shop (no. 95) reads 'Robinson, Provision Dealer'.

72. Will Smith in front of his newsagent's shop, no. 28 Wigan Lane, *c.*1905. Later, he bought no. 26 as well. Smith was famous for his collection and reproduction of postcards, for which he was nicknamed the 'Postcard King'. This shop still survives as a newsagent's.

73. The paper boy, with his bell, 1891.

74.   The fish hawker, 1891.

75.  Mrs. Haworth outside her house in Boyswell Lane, Scholes. An advertisement in the window mentions horehound pop and beer – homemade. Her daughter has added under the photograph, 'my mother, God Bless her; no fancy dress, but she was a lady!'

76.   The hot potato boy, Woodhouse Lane, 1891.

77.  The rag and bone man, Woodhouse Lane, 1891.

78.   The greengrocer, Woodhouse Lane, 1891.

79.   The Manor House, Scholes, 1887. On the left of the picture is John Blinkhorn's clogger's shop. John McQuaid, a Wigan councillor, owned the grocer's shop (no. 147); he also had a shop in nearby Wellington Street. The butcher's shop belonged to William Hall – the standard of hygiene left a lot to be desired!

80.  William Christopher, travelling butcher, 1891. At this time, he had premises at no. 11 Woodhouse Lane; this photograph was taken further along the road, beside the *Belle Vue*. Until recently, he had operated from his house at no. 52 Millgate.

81.  Walter Patterson's oyster saloon and supper bar, no.3 Coopers Row, *c.*1903. Patterson also had a stall on the fish market.

82. Billhead, Marsh & Pendlebury, no. 7 Standishgate, 1867. A few months later, the firm became John Pendlebury. In 1878, he moved to new premises lower down Standishgate and, by 1885, had acquired nos. 17-23; in 1949 Pendlebury's sold out to Debenhams. No. 7 Standishgate was bought by Evans and McClure, drapers.

83. Meek's Cellars in Rowbottom Square, off Wallgate, c.1910. George Bond specialised in the sale of fents (remnants of cloth). His shop was only a small part of Meek's Buildings at nos. 17-19 Wallgate. This once prestigious shop had been built by Joseph Meek, linen draper and silk mercer, in the mid-1850s, and Lady Crawford was a regular customer. Joseph Meek & Sons went into liquidation in 1884.

84.  Mrs. Woosey's grocer's shop, *c.*1900. This
shop was at no. 43 Scholes, on the corner of
Warrington Lane. Next door, at no. 45, was
Miss McDonald, wardrobe dealer.

85. Makinson Arcade, looking towards Standishgate, 1913. Opened in 1898, this was Wigan's largest and most elaborate arcade. The decorations are in celebration of the visit of King George V (*see* photograph 136). The shirt-sleeved shopkeeper on the left is William Millard, who had set up his own photographic business in the arcade. His studio is now a jeweller's. Signs for Wilson's mantles and Heap's Dining Room can be seen.

86.  The Market Place, 1826, from a contemporary water-colour by Thomas Whitehouse of Wigan. The building on the left is the Moot Hall, rebuilt around this time and demolished in 1869. On the right is the New Town Hall, built in 1720, and demolished in 1882 to make way for street improvements. The building next but one to the Moot Hall is the *Black Horse* (*see* photograph 88).

87.  The New Town Hall, *c.*1870. The upper portion, which houses the council chamber, had a turret, a large stone badge portraying the original arms of George I, and a railed balcony from which many political speeches were delivered in the days of the old hustings. The ground floor was called the 'Shambles', and was occupied entirely by butchers' shops.

88. Market Place, looking south, *c*.1910. Lowe's had opened in 1887, and later expanded at the expense of two adjoining taverns, the *White Lion* and the *Bulls Head*; a third public house, the *Black Horse*, is to the left of Lowe's. In 1985, however, the business closed, just two years short of its centenary.

89. Market Place, looking north, *c*.1895. The steam tram is taking on water, a very frequent occurrence. Some familiar names can be seen here, including O. & G. Rushton and Lipton (grocers), Salter & Salter, Wallace & Co. and Craddock Brothers (boot manufacturers). Between Wallace's and Craddock's was the *Kings Head*, appropriately the meeting place of the Wigan Master Cloggers' Association.

90.   Market Place, 1898, just before Library Street was opened up. The premises of Atherton and Gould and Daniel Barlow (nos. 1 and 3 Market Place respectively) were about to be demolished to make way for it – notices in the latter's window refer to a closing-down sale. The Manchester and County Bank (no. 5 Market Place) and Coop's shop (nos. 1 and 3 Wallgate) remained.

91.  Wallgate, looking north, 1892. The premises on the left are now occupied by the Royal Bank of Scotland, while the building with the triangular frontage (dating from 1884) is today the Yorkshire Bank. The Post Office was also opened in 1884 (its fourth site in the Wallgate area in 24 years!). The well-known *Dog and Partridge*, dating from the 18th century, is now the *Bees Knees*.

92.  Wallgate, looking south, *c*.1900. A station had been opened here by the Lancashire and Yorkshire Railway Company in 1848; the present Wallgate station was built in 1896. The *Victoria Hotel*, opened in 1894, was built on the site of an earlier hostelry of the same name.

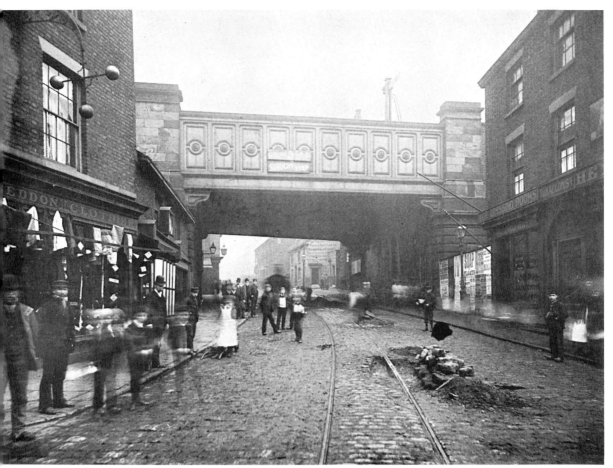

93. Wallgate Bridge, *c*.1890. The shops on the left (nos. 98 and 100) belonged to John Seddon – one was a pawnbroker's and clothier's, the other a watchmaker's (notice the clock above the shop). On the right are Stephen Taylor's 'London Haircutting Saloon' and John Heywood's tobacconist's and grocer's shop. Through the bridge can be seen the *Swan and Railway Hotel* (left) and the *Railway Inn* (right).

94. A Wigan Tramways Co. steam tram, probably at the foot of Wallgate, *c*.1890. Notice the light roof on the upper deck. The first steam tram in Wigan ran in 1880, and the last 24 years later.

95. Market Street, January 1902.
Originally, the top of the street, down to
the *Crofters' Arms*, had been part of
Hallgate. The interesting hoardings hide
the rebuilding of the shops at the corner
of Market Street and Market Place.
Unlike the *Crofters' Arms*, the buildings
on the right-hand side have not survived.

96. The Market Hall, looking from Market Street, *c.*1890. Opened on 21 May 1877, at a total cost of £40,000, Wigan's first covered market saw the removal of the stalls which had long impeded the traffic, 'to the infinite satisfaction of pedestrians and horsemen'. The Market Square 'is considered one of the finest squares ... for the wholesale business ... of any town in the kingdom'.

97. A fish shop, Hallgate, just round the corner from Market Street. This is now occupied by 'Memory Lane'. On the right is Jack Millard, one of the sons of James Millard, the famous Wigan photographer. Jack became a sculptor of considerable note, and was to make a bust of his father.

98.  James Millard outside his studio in Market Street, *c.*1900. A man of many talents, he built the studio, on the site now occupied by the Queen's Hall, himself, and sculptured the statues of the pit-brow lassie and the mill girl in 1895. This photograph was probably taken by his son William, who followed in his father's footsteps (*see* photograph 85).

99. Standishgate, looking north from Market Place, *c*.1891. This photograph was taken before the advent of tramlines in the street. On the right is the famous *Royal Hotel* (no. 1 Standishgate); the site is now occupied by John Menzies. The splendid building in the centre, no. 4 Standishgate, was Parr's Bank (now the National Westminster).

100. Mabs Cross, Standishgate, 1892. In 1921, this was moved across the road. On the extreme left is the *Golden Cross*. The large house in the centre was owned by James Smith, slate and coal merchant, and mayor of Wigan 1889-90; a surgeon, John Webster, lived next door. Out of picture was the *Green Man*, of which photographer John Cooper had once been landlord.

101.  The postman, 1891.

102.  Dr. James White outside his home, no. 139 Wigan Lane, in 1892. Dr. White was for a time surgeon at the Dispensary, and indeed actually lived for a number of years in King Street. This house, at the corner of Wigan Lane and New Lodge, was of course much closer to the Infirmary, where he moved on its opening in 1873 (*see* photograph 109).

103.  The chimney-sweep, 1891.

104.   Mr. Wickham's drawing room, *c.*1898. Leaning against the wall is his double-bass, with which he used to accompany the congregational singing before the church was built. On the wall are a number of his own photographs.

105.   No. 2 Coppull Lane on 26 March 1886, after a gas explosion which killed three and injured six passers-by. Ironically, the house did not use gas! The local newspaper reported that the front of the house had been 'completely cut out as effectually as if it had been taken out by a builder', and referred to Mr. Wragg's 'excellent photograph'.

106. Wigan Dispensary building, King Street. From its opening in 1801, subscribers could recommend one out-patient for treatment for every half-guinea subscribed. There were never any facilities for in-patient care. From 1827, the staff comprised a resident house surgeon, matron, and three honorary surgeons. The Dispensary closed in 1876 and the building became a savings bank; today, it is Wigan Metropolitan Borough Council's Rates Office.

107. Royal Albert Edward Infirmary out-patients' waiting hall, c.1920. Even for an out-patient, admission, as in the Dispensary, was largely by recommendation only, on the basis of one for every half-guinea subscribed; a subscriber could recommend one in-patient for every two guineas of his subscription.

108.  The proposed Royal Albert Edward Infirmary, 1873. Opened by the Prince and Princess of Wales, it had completely superseded the Dispensary by 1876. The male and female wings were to the right and left of the Administrative Offices, with the surgery and casualty departments behind. There was ward accommodation for 45 males and 15 women. In 1877, a children's ward was opened.

109.  Surgeons and staff of the Royal Albert Edward Infirmary, *c*.1875. There were five honorary surgeons, all legally registered, one of whom had to be in attendance each day. Dr. White (*see* photograph 102) is standing (*left*); seated (*right*) is Dr. Berry, who was to become Medical Officer of Health for Wigan. In the centre is Miss McIntyre, the matron, who was responsible for the domestic management of the hospital.

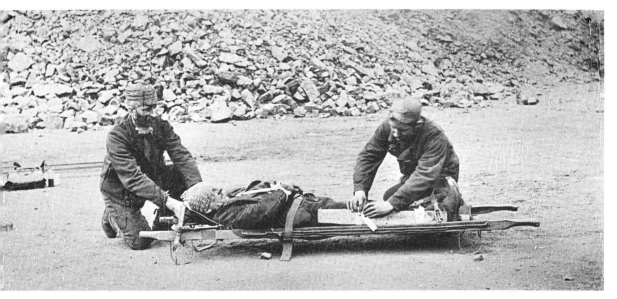

10. A mining accident in 1891 – these were all too frequent. Three years earlier, Mr. Wickham had referred to 'a shocking headgear accident at the Douglas Bank Colliery, in which five men were killed'. Recommendations for admission to the Infirmary were not always essential in cases of accident or emergency.

11. Wigan's first horse-ambulance, a gift to the Infirmary in 1889. Initially, it was the responsibility of the patient or his family to find transport to the Infirmary. This ambulance, however, had to be available to the public at all times, for the transmission of casualties. By 1893, the area between Skelmersdale and Atherton was served by 19 such vehicles.

# ROYAL ALBERT EDWARD INFIRMARY & DISPENSARY.

## MEDICAL REPORT

*For the year ending March 31st, 1875.*

Number of Beds in Men's Medical Wards ..................... 15

„          „          „        Surgical Wards .................... 20

„          „          „     Women's Wards ............................. 15

Total number of Beds...... 50

*GENERAL STATEMENT of the In and Out-patients under treatment during the year :—*

### IN-PATIENTS.

Admitted during the year :          TOTAL.

Medical ........................... 42 } 170
Surgical ........................... 128 }

Discharged cured and relieved :

Medical ........................... 29 } 114
Surgical ........................... 85 }

Discharged unrelieved :

Medical ........................... 4 } 11
Surgical ........................... 7 }

Died :

Medical ........................... 0 } 11
Surgical ........................... 11 }

Admitted in a dying condition........ 6

Remaining April 1st, 1875 :

Medical ........................... 5 } 28
Surgical ........................... 23 }

Number of *post-mortem* examinations........ 3

### OUT-PATIENTS.

Admitted during the year .....................2612

Visited at their own homes ..................... 670

### OCCUPATION OF IN-PATIENTS.

| | | | | | |
|---|---|---|---|---|---|
| Agents | 1 | Charwomen | 1 | Locksmiths | 1 |
| Bakers | 1 | Colliers, Sinkers,&c. | 49 | Milliners | 1 |
| Brewers Servants | 2 | Domestic Servants | 6 | Plumbers, Painters | 2 |
| Brass Moulders | 3 | Factory Hands | 25 | Railway Servants | 3 |
| Bricklayers | 1 | Gas Fitters | 1 | Scholars | 7 |
| Brickmakers | 2 | Hawkers | 2 | Tailors | 3 |
| Butchers | 2 | Horse Dealers | 2 | Various, Wives, &c. | 41 |
| Carpenters | 2 | Labourers | 12 | | |

112. Wigan Infirmary Medical report, 1875. One thousand patients per year had been expected in the new Infirmary, a far cry from the 2,612 out-patients and 170 in-patients admitted in 1875. By 1877, these numbers had risen to 4,388 and 459! Five years later, 782 in-patients were admitted.

# Report of Cases for the Year Ending March 31st, 1875.

## GENERAL DISEASES.

Erysipelas ..................... 3
Rheumatism ................... 4
Gout ........................... 1
Cancer ....................... 5
Tumours ..................... 1
Scrofula .. ..................... 3
Phthisis ............... ......... 5
Anœmia...................... 3

## NERVOUS DISEASES.

Paralysis ..................... 8
Epilepsy ................... .. 3
Chorea ....................... 1
Hysteria...... ............... 2
Locomoter Ataxia ........... 1
Neuralgia .................... 1

## CIRCULATORY SYSTEM.

Diseases of Heart.......... 3
Aneurism ..................... 1
Gangrene .................... 1

## RESPIRATORY SYSTEM.

Bronchitis .................... 3
Pneumonia ... .............. 3

## DIGESTIVE SYSTEM.

Dyspepsia .................... 1
Hernia ...................... 3
Jaundice .................... 1
Tabes Mesenterica ......... 1
Cirrhosis of Liver........... 1
Inflammation of Liver ...... 2
General Anasarea............ 1

## ABSORBENT SYSTEM.

Bronchocele .................. 1

## ORGANS OF LOCOMOTION.

Disease of bones ........... 9
   „        joints ...........12

## INJURIES.

Concussion of Brain... ..... 1
Injuries to Back ........... 4
Burns......................... 3
Sprains ....................... 4
Contusions.................... 9
Wounds... ...... ............ 8
Fracture of Skull .......... 1
   „        Ribs ........... 1
   „        Thigh ........ 3
   „  .     Leg ........... 8
Compound fracture of Thigh 1
   „         „     Finger 1
   „         „     Leg ... 1
   „  Dislocation of wrist 1

## NOT CLASSIFIED.

Diseases of the skin ......... 3
Ulcers .....................21
Abscess ...................... 9
Diseases of Bursæ ........... 2
Sinus ........................ 3

113. (*left*) The victim of a mining accident at Douglas Bank Colliery in 1891. Nearly half the Infirmary's in-patients were colliers.

114. (*below*) Rylance Row, off Standishgate, *c*.1900, just before demolition. This ran parallel to, and just south of, Dicconson Street. Note the bulging walls and primitive gutterings and downspouts. Incredibly, a number of these houses were common lodging houses; the 1881 census records that one of them had 20 occupants – a husband and wife, three daughters, one son, and 14 lodgers!

115. (*right*) The knocker-upper, once a very familiar character, employed by the colliery or factory to wake up its employees each morning.

116. (*below*) A typical scene off Woodhouse Lane, 1891.

117.   The scene behind the *Roebuck* (now McDonalds), off Standishgate, *c.*1900. The property shown here was pulled down in 1910 and the *Roebuck* closed in 1942.

118.   Millstone Yard, off Wigan Lane, November 1902. This photograph was taken from the *Millstone*, which still survives it faces onto Wigan Lane directly opposite Charles Street.

119.  Collier washing, 1891.

120.   Collier having his 'baggin', 1891.

121.  The bread oven, 1891.

122.  Scrubbing steps, 1891.

123. Dolly-tub and peg, 1891.

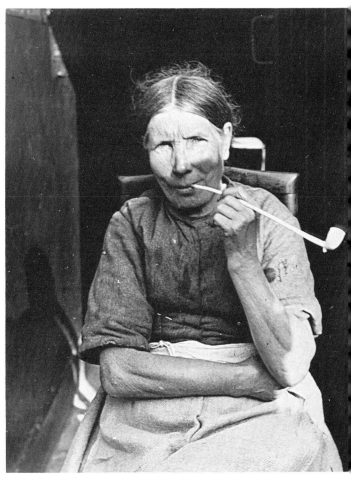

124. Smoking the pipe, 1891.

125. Collier 'keawring' or squatting (probably derived from cowering), 1891.

126.   Washday in the alley, 1891.

127.   Faggy Lane, off Chapel Lane, 1900. The
railway ran virtually alongside, to the right.

128. (*right*) Little London, off Standishgate, just north of Dicconson Terrace, *c*.1900. This area became particularly heavily populated around this time.

129. (*below*) Plantation Gates, Wigan Lane, *c*.1895. Haigh was one of the first estates in the country to allow free access to pedestrians (apart from on the first Monday of October, to preserve ownership rights). The lodgekeeper in the photograph is James Higson, an old soldier, who was a familiar figure in the area for a quarter of a century, until his death in 1898.

130. Wigan Excelsior Cycling Club outside the entrance to Garswood Hall while on a summer rally in 1898.

131. James Millard outside his home at no. 119 Victoria Street, Newtown, with his wife Susannah and daughter Beatrice in the doorway, *c*.1905. He moved here in 1902, on his retirement, which lasted for 28 years. He constructed the pedal cycle and sidecar himself!

132. St Paul's Congregational church choir picnic to Matlock, 1896.

133. Excursion about to set off from *Woodhouses Inn*, Woodhouse Lane, *c*.1895. This was the nearest tavern to the Douglas Bank Colliery.

# WIGAN & DISTRICT SUNDAY SCHOOL UNION.

## GENERAL HOLIDAY, JUNE 19, 1895.

The Committee of the above have arranged with the L. & N.-W. Railway to run a

## SPECIAL EXCURSION TO

# CHESTER, ❖ HOLYWELL, ❖ RHYL,

# COLWYN BAY,

# LLANDUDNO

AND

# BETTWYS-Y-COED.

FARES FOR THE DOUBLE JOURNEY:

Chester **2/3.**   Holywell and Rhyl **3/-.**   Llandudno and Colwyn
Bay **3/6.**   Bettwys-y-Coed **4/-.**   Children under 12 Half-price.

## TRAIN LEAVES

Wigan (L. & N.-W.) for Llandudno at 5-55 a.m., for Bettwys-y-Coed at 6-0.
Bamfurlong ,, ,, 6-0 ,, ,, 6-5.
Golborne ,, ,, 6-10 ,, ,, 6-15.
BOTH TRAINS WILL CALL AT ALL OTHER STATIONS NAMED ABOVE.
RETURNING from Bettwys-y-Coed at 6-30 p.m., Llandudno at 7-15 p.m., Colwyn Bay at 7-30 p.m.,
Rhyl at 7-50 p.m , Holywell at 8-15 p m., Chester at 8-55 p.m.

SPECIAL.---Arrangements have been made with the Proprietors of the
Steamship "ST. TUDNO," for passengers by this Excursion to be con-
veyed from Llandudno to Menai Bridge and back, at the Single Fares for
the Double Journey, viz:---Saloon, 2/-; 2nd, 1/6; on production of Coupon
which will be given with the Railway Ticket on application.

34. Wigan and District Sunday School Union organised talks and exhibitions, and ran special children's excursions. On
his occasion, nearly 1,000 went to Wales; most went straight to Llandudno, and many saw the sea for the first time. The
General Holiday, on a Wednesday in June, was by now well established, and saw a virtually complete exodus from the town
o the sea.

135. (*right*) Lancashire Fire
Brigade's Friendly Society
demonstration in Market Square,
June 1890. The society,
inaugurated in 1877 to provide
relief to disabled firemen and
grants to widows, met each year in
a member town. In 1890, Wigan
was host and so first in the
procession through the town. Both
the brigade's steam engines were
out, and can be seen nearest the
camera.

136. (*below*) Visit of King George V
and Queen Mary to Wigan, 10 July
1913. The King is seen here in front
of the Market Hall. This was part
of an eight-day tour of Lancashire,
during which the royal couple
stayed at Knowsley Hall. One
night, they were entertained by
George Formby; unfortunately,
'the Lancashire dialect appeared
slightly to puzzle their Majesties'.

137. The Prince of Wales leaving the Lancashire and Yorkshire Railway Station, 18 May 1898. The Prince had been inspecting the Lancashire Hussars in Southport. He then travelled by road to Garswood Hall, where he was staying as guest of Lord Gerard. Exactly 25 years earlier, the Prince had opened the Royal Albert Edward Infirmary.

138. The marriage of James Henry Marsden to Sarah Ellen Waterworth, 30 July 1898. This photograph was taken at the Hollies, Wigan Lane. The bride and groom are standing between their respective sisters (dressed in white); the groom's mother-in-law has wasted no time in making her presence felt!

139. Presentation of the Freedom of the Borough to Andrew Carnegie, LL.D., 29 May 1909. Five years earlier, he had donated £5,000 towards the cost of building Pemberton Library, and he had contributed generously to the Maypole Colliery Disaster Fund. He was presented with a silver casket, inset with views of Pemberton Library, the Maypole Colliery, Wigan Infirmary and the parish church.

140. (*left*) Wigan Public Library reference department, 1900. The building was designed by Alfred Waterhouse and presented to the Corporation by Thomas Taylor in October 1877. In May 1878, the new library was opened to the public. It opened on Sundays, one of only three such libraries in the country. In 1880, there were over 10,500 Sunday users!

141. (*below*) Wigan Public Library staff, 1898. In the centre is the borough librarian, Henry Folkard.

142.   Pemberton Colliery School rugby league team, 1912. For many years this school boasted the leading team in the area. On the right is yet another son of James Millard – George, a teacher and, later, liaison officer for various rugby league teams on tour in France.

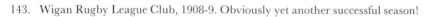

143.   Wigan Rugby League Club, 1908-9. Obviously yet another successful season!

144. (*left*) Tennis at Gidlow Lodge, *c.*1890.

145. (*below*) Wigan Swimming and Water Polo Club, 1909. The display of trophies is impressive enough but, on the back of this postcard, an avid supporter has written, 'Our team – Champions of the World!'

146. (*above*) The *Douglas Tavern* at the
corner of Chapel Lane and Douglas
Street, *c.*1900. The days of this hostelry
were numbered – when the licence came
up for renewal, there were police
objections, on the grounds that 'the
building was hardly fit for a dwelling
house, never mind a public house'. The
tavern was closed soon afterwards.

147. (*right*) The *Bricklayers' Arms*, no. 29
Hallgate. This tavern, which dates back
to the early 19th century, still survives.

148.   The *Harp Inn*, at the corner of Scholes and Vauxhall Road, *c.*1900. At this time, there was a public house at virtually every street corner in Scholes.

149.   The *Horseshoe Inn*, no. 106 Millgate, in 1892 when Giles Westhead was landlord. This 18th-century public house belonged to a number of breweries, including James Fairhurst Ltd., the Knotty Ash Brewery, and Higsons and Burtonwood The posters are advertising various church functions and summer excursions to Blackpool.

150. (*above*) The *Beehive*, Wigan Lane, c.1900. This was a Burton Brewery house which closed in 1907.

151. (*right*) The *Big Lamp Hotel*, no. 7 Wallgate, c.1880. This was for a time between two other hostelries. On the left was the *Raven*, which can be partly seen here and is still a familiar Wigan landmark. The *Big Lamp* was soon to be taken over by the *Golden Lion* on the other side, an 18th-century inn which closed in 1969.

152. A Wigan and District Tramways Co. steam tram in Ormskirk Road, on the Wigan-Newton-Pemberton route, *c*.1900.

153. The *Minorca Hotel*, at the corner of Wallgate and King Street, dates from the 18th century and enjoyed a high reputation for its food as well as its ale. Originally a Robinson's house, it was one of 35 Wigan houses taken over by Magee Marshall in 1894.

## ❖ MENU ❖

Turtle Soup.    White Soup.

---

Salmon and Cucumber.
Filleted Soles.    Shrimp Sauce.

---

Oyster Patties.
Sweetbread with Sauce Piquante.
Chicken Croquettes.    Broiled Mushrooms.

---

Sirloin Beef.    Boiled Chickens.
Tongue.
Haunch of Venison.
Pheasants.    Woodcocks.

---

Cabinet Pudding.    Orange Jelly.
Meringues á la Crême.
Calves' Feet Jelly.    Tartlets.    Apricot Jam.
Raspberry Crême.    Ices.

---

Fondue.

---

DESSERT.

## ❖ TOASTS ❖

| Proposed by | Toasts | Response by |
|---|---|---|
| THE PRESIDENT - - | - THE QUEEN AND ROYAL - FAMILY | ............ |
| J. WHITE, ESQ. - - | THE BISHOP AND CLERGY OF THE DIOCESE | ............ |
| E. H. MONKS, ESQ., J.P. | - THE ARMY, NAVY, AND - RESERVE FORCES | SURGEON TATHAM |
| R. PATRICK, ESQ. - | - THE WIGAN MEDICAL - SOCIETY | THE PRESIDENT |
| W. ROOCROFT, ESQ., J.P. | - - - THE VISITORS - - - | J. E. SCOWCROFT, ESQ. |
| R. WILLIAMS, ESQ. | - - THE LADIES - - - | W. MITCHELL ROOCROFT, ESQ. |
| J. B. STUART, ESQ. - | OFFICERS OF THE SOCIETY | R. P. WHITE, ESQ. |
| R. F. WOODCOCK, ESQ. | THE DINNER COMMITTEE | W. BERRY, ESQ., J.P. |

154.   Menu for the Wigan Medical Society annual dinner at the *Victoria Hotel*, Wallgate, February 1884. The cost was 10s. 6d. each, plus wine. The society was founded in 1875 and all registered medical practitioners within a radius of seven miles of Wigan were eligible to join. Meetings were held monthly, at which papers were read and particular cases discussed.

155.   Barnes' restaurant at no. 52 Market Street was a popular eating house for many years.

156.  (*above*) The Byers Orchestra, *c.*1905. This was named after its founder, Charles Byers, and played at many concerts in the town.

157.  (*left*) The *Old Dog*, Coopers Row, off Market Place, 1908. This comprised a public house and music hall. Behind the *Old Dog* was the Alexandra Hall (Wigan's first purpose-built music hall), which became the Empire Palace in 1892. Performers there included Vesta Tilley, Madame Petti and Will Fyffe. It later became a cinema, then a bingo hall, before finally being demolished in 1978.

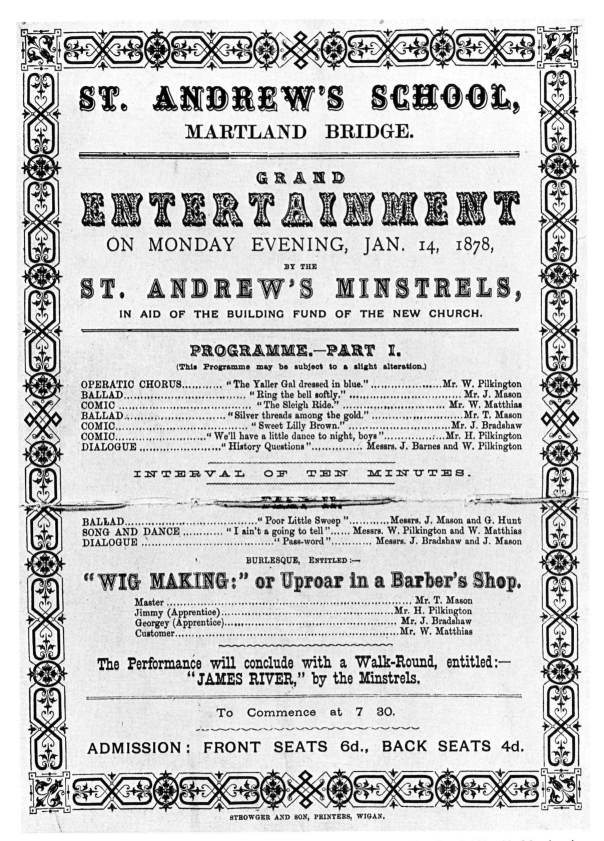

# ST. ANDREW'S SCHOOL,
## MARTLAND BRIDGE.

### GRAND
# ENTERTAINMENT
## ON MONDAY EVENING, JAN. 14, 1878,
#### BY THE
# ST. ANDREW'S MINSTRELS,
### IN AID OF THE BUILDING FUND OF THE NEW CHURCH.

## PROGRAMME.—PART I.
#### (This Programme may be subject to a slight alteration.)

OPERATIC CHORUS........... "The Yaller Gal dressed in blue." .....................Mr. W. Pilkington
BALLAD................................... "Ring the bell softly." ............................... Mr. J. Mason
COMIC ....................................... "The Sleigh Ride." ............................... Mr. W. Matthias
BALLAD................................... "Silver threads among the gold." ........................... Mr. T. Mason
COMIC...................................... "Sweet Lilly Brown." ...............................Mr. J. Bradshaw
COMIC.................................."We'll have a little dance to night, boys "...............Mr. H. Pilkington
DIALOGUE ,...................,...."History Questions ".............. Messrs. J. Barnes and W. Pilkington

### INTERVAL OF TEN MINUTES.

BALLAD................................"Poor Little Sweep "...........Messrs. J. Mason and G. Hunt
SONG AND DANCE ,........... "I ain't a going to tell"...... Messrs. W. Pilkington and W. Matthias
DIALOGUE ..................................."Pass-word "........... Messrs. J. Bradshaw and J. Mason

#### BURLESQUE, ENTITLED :—

# "WIG MAKING:" or Uproar in a Barber's Shop.

Master ............................................................. Mr. T. Mason
Jimmy (Apprentice)............................................Mr. H. Pilkington
Georgey (Apprentice)....................................... Mr. J. Bradshaw
Customer........................................................Mr. W. Matthias

### The Performance will conclude with a Walk-Round, entitled:—
### "JAMES RIVER," by the Minstrels.

## To Commence at 7 30.

# ADMISSION: FRONT SEATS 6d., BACK SEATS 4d.

STROWGER AND SON, PRINTERS, WIGAN.

158. Grand Entertainment, St Andrew's School, 1878. This was one of many functions held in aid of the church building fund.

159. The Empress Ballroom, Station Road. Opened on 1 November 1916, it had a dancing area of 71ft. by 54ft., and a spectator gallery and supper room. In 1926 a new annexe was built, the Palais-de-Dance. The ballroom was originally owned by the Atherton Brothers (*see* photograph 64). In 1965, it became nationally famous as Wigan Casino. It was demolished in 1984.

160. The Pavilion, Library Street, was opened in March 1909. It was owned by the famous Worswick family. The first act was the Minnehaha Amateur Minstrels, a charity show to provide clogs and stockings for poor children. In the 1920s, it became a cinema, the Picturedrome. The building, which occupied the Library Street section of the present Wigan Baths, was demolished in 1959.

**PROGRAMME**

# Royal Court Theatre

## WIGAN

**JOHN WORSWICK** — Proprietor & Manager

OPEN EVERY EVENING AT 6·30
SATURDAY AT 6·15
TELEPHONE 0394

THE GEM THEATRE of LANCASHIRE

161. The Royal Court Theatre was built in 1886 by John Worswick, the famous Wigan theatre manager, and landlord of the *Shakespeare* opposite. Among those appearing in the early years were Henry Irving, Fred Karno, Keir Hardy, Ramsey MacDonald and General Booth. In 1931, the auditorium became the Court Cinema and the Court Hall next door became the Court Ballroom. Today, the Royal Court is a bingo club.

*The Wigan Archives Service*

Presently based in Leigh Town Hall and part of Wigan's Department of Leisure, the Service is responsible for the preservation of manuscript and photographic material relating to Metropolitan Wigan. Its collections are available to the public in the Record Office searchroom, 10.00 a.m.-4.00 p.m., Monday to Friday; an appointment is advisable (0942-672421 ext.266). The Archivist is keen to hear from those who have local archives or photographs in their possession. The item, if not donated, can be copied and the original returned within days. It is only through such co-operation that a record of Wigan's heritage can be preserved and a book such as this produced.